In Memory of

Roger E. Allen

Presented by His Loving
Wife & Children

Mary Allen

Brad Allen

Nancy Talarico

Betsy Jones

2005

Buddy BOOKS
Prehistoric Animals

Saber-toothed Cat

ABDO
Publishing Company

A Buddy Book
by
Michael P. Goecke

VISIT US AT

www.abdopub.com

Published by Buddy Books, an imprint of ABDO Publishing Company, 4940 Viking Drive, Edina, Minnesota 55435. Copyright © 2003 by Abdo Consulting Group, Inc. International copyrights reserved in all countries. No part of this book may be reproduced in any form without written permission from the publisher.

Printed in the United States.

Edited by: Christy DeVillier
Contributing Editor: Matt Ray
Graphic Design: Deborah Coldiron
Image Research: Deborah Coldiron
Illustrations: Deborah Coldiron, Denise Esner
Photographs: Corbis, Fotosearch, Steve McHugh, Photodisc

Library of Congress Cataloging-in-Publication Data

Goecke, Michael P., 1968-
    Saber-toothed cat / Michael P. Goecke.
        p. cm. -- (Prehistoric animals Set I)
    Includes index.
    Summary: Introduces the physical characteristics, habitat, and behavior of the prehistoric relative of modern-day African lions.
        ISBN 1-57765-970-8
    1. Smilodon—Juvenile literature. [1. Saber-toothed tigers.] I. Title.

QE882.C15 G64 2003
569'.75—dc21

                                                                2002028194

Table of Contents

Prehistoric Animals

Scientists believe Earth is more than four billion years old. Long before people, many kinds of plants and animals lived here.

Animals that lived more than 5,500 years ago are called prehistoric. Dinosaurs, woolly mammoths, and saber-toothed cats are all prehistoric animals.

Prehistoric Animals

Saber-toothed Cats

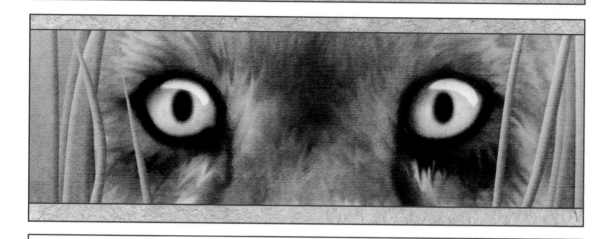

Smilodon
(SMY-luh-don)

Scientists study **fossils** to learn about the world long ago. Fossils help them understand **prehistoric** animals like saber-toothed cats.

People have dug up many saber-toothed cat fossils in California. More than 2,000 came from the Rancho La Brea Tar Pits.

Saber-toothed cats were named for their large, knife-sized teeth. There were more than 35 kinds of saber-toothed cats. Some were as big as lions. Others were the size of large house cats.

Saber-toothed cats lived everywhere except Antarctica and Australia. They were around for about 40 million years.

The Smilodon

The largest saber-toothed cats were *Smilodons*. These prehistoric cats lived in North America and South America. They were deadly predators.

A Map Of The World

North America

South America

Smilodon fossils have been found in North America and South America.

The *Smilodon* could roar like today's lions.

The *Smilodon* is a member of the cat family, Felidae. These big cats could roar like today's lions. But *Smilodons* are not closely related to today's cats.

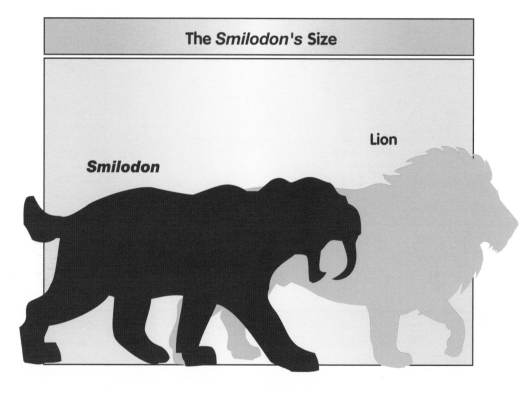

The *Smilodon*'s Size

Smilodon

Lion

Adult *Smilodons* were about as big as today's lions. They grew to become more than three feet (one m) tall. They may have weighed about 500 pounds (227 kg).

A fossil of the *Smilodon*'s head and large teeth.

All saber-toothed cats had two extra-large canine teeth. They curved downward from the cat's upper jaw. These large teeth could grow to become as long as seven inches (eighteen cm).

The *Smilodon* was a deadly predator.

Like most cats, the *Smilodon* had fur all over. Its tail was short like a bobcat's tail. The *Smilodon's* short legs were thick and strong. This saber-toothed cat also had a strong mouth for biting.

Smilodons were the biggest saber-toothed cats.

Retractable Claws

Most kinds of cats have retractable claws. Retractable claws are hidden inside a cat's paws. But they can be seen when cats use them for scratching. Scientists believe that the *Smilodon* had retractable claws, too.

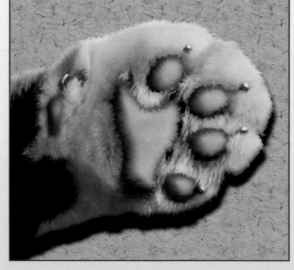

Retractable claws stay hidden until cats use them.

Prides

African lions today live in groups, or prides. Members of a lion pride sometimes hunt together. They share food with the rest of the pride. This allows hurt lions to heal before hunting again.

A pride of lions.

Did *Smilodons* also live in prides? Scientists study *Smilodon* fossils to answer this question. Many *Smilodon* fossils show wounds that have healed. Some scientists believe a hurt *Smilodon* would die on its own. They think these saber-toothed cats healed with help from a pride.

Smilodons probably hunted horses, bison, and young elephants. Scientists believe Smilodons ambushed their prey. Ambush hunters sneak up behind prey. They also hide quietly and wait for prey to come near. This helps them take animals by surprise.

Young elephants were probably food for Smilodons.

17

Saber-toothed cats probably used their large canine teeth to kill prey. Maybe they killed by biting and holding on. Struggles with animals may have broken the *Smilodon's* teeth.

Most *Smilodon* fossils do not have broken canine teeth. So, some scientists believe *Smilodons* killed another way. Maybe they bit an animal's neck or soft belly. Animals would die from these wounds.

Saber-toothed cats probably killed prey
with their large canine teeth.

Scientists have names for important time periods in Earth's history. *Smilodons* lived during a time period called the Pleistocene. The Pleistocene began about two million years ago.

A Geologic Timeline
248 Million Years Ago – Today

Triassic 248 – 213 Million Years Ago	Jurassic 213 – 145 Million Years Ago	Cretaceous 145 – 65 Million Years Ago	Paleocene 65 – 56 Million Years Ago	Eocene 56 – 34 Million Years Ago	Oligocene 34 – 24 Million Years Ago	Miocene 24 – 5 Million Years Ago	Pliocene 5 – 2 Million Years Ago	Pleistocene 2 Million – 11,500 Years Ago	Holocene 11,500 Years Ago – Today

Age Of Dinosaurs 248 – 65 Million Years Ago	Age Of Mammals 65 Million Years Ago – Today

Smilodons lived between one and a half million and 10,000 years ago.

20

The Pleistocene Ice Age

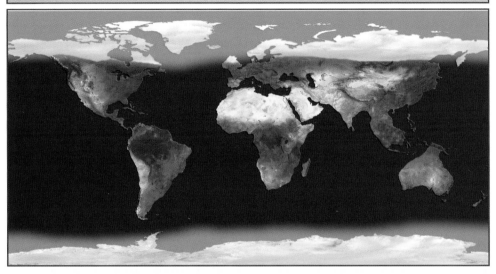

Ice covered parts of the world during the Ice Age.

The last Ice Age took place during the Pleistocene. During that time, the world cooled. Giant sheets of ice covered many lands. Mammoths, giant sloths, giant apes, and rhinos lived during the Ice Age, too.

Smilodons died out near the end of the Ice Age. This happened about 11,500 years ago. Other animals died out around the same time. Scientists are not sure why this happened.

Maybe illness killed Smilodon and other Ice Age animals. Maybe they died from a great climate change. Did early humans have something to do with it? Scientists are working hard to uncover this great mystery.

Important Words

ambush hiding in order to surprise prey.

canine teeth sharp and pointed teeth. Most animals have four canine teeth.

climate the weather of a place over time.

fossil remains of very old animals and plants commonly found in the ground. A fossil can be a bone, a footprint, or any trace of life.

predator an animal that hunts and eats other animals.

prehistoric describes anything that was around more than 5,500 years ago.

prey an animal that is food for another animal.

Web Sites

To learn more about saber-toothed cats, visit ABDO Publishing Company on the World Wide Web. Web sites about saber-toothed cats are featured on our Book Links page. These links are routinely monitored and updated to provide the most current information available.

www.abdopub.com

23

Index